Name: ....

Class: ....

School: ....

Digraphs

mimic
laptop
sank
neck
magpie
rapid

quench
outing
rescue
jumped
disagree
correct

mushroom
raincoat
spoilsport
backyard
swimming
thunderstorm

Put the words in the spelling list into alphabetical order.

1. _____ 10. _____
2. _____ 11. _____
3. _____ 12. _____
4. _____ 13. _____
5. _____ 14. _____
6. _____ 15. _____
7. _____ 16. _____
8. _____ 17. _____
9. _____ 18. _____

Look up each word in the dictionary and read its definition. Write the page number in the storm cloud.

quench   mimic   rescue

neck   sank   waist

Listen for the vowels in the words and decide whether they are long or short. Put a ‹⌣› over the letters making the short vowels and ‹—› or ‹— •› over the letters making the long ones.

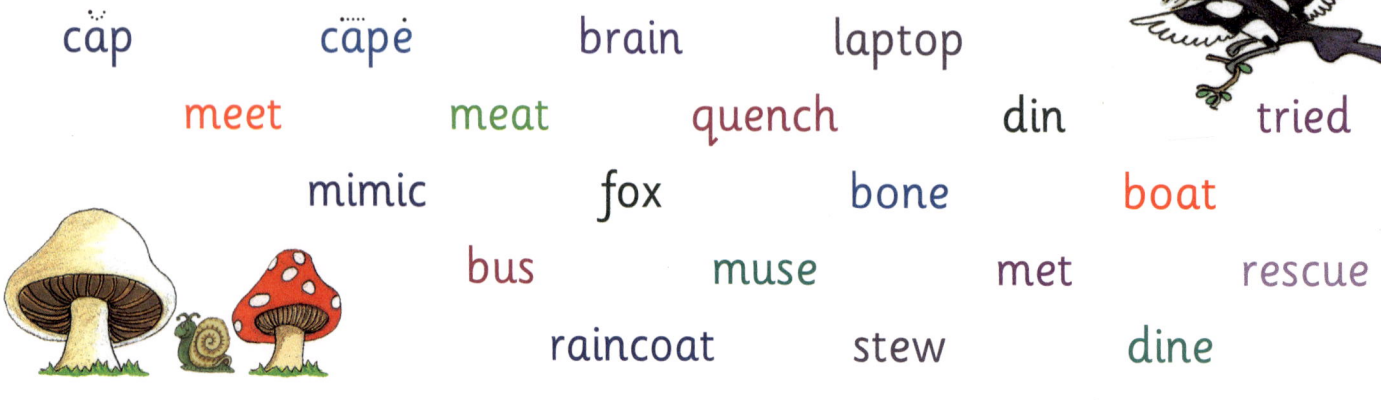

căp   cāpē   brain   laptop

meet   meat   quench   din   tried

mimic   fox   bone   boat

bus   muse   met   rescue

raincoat   stew   dine

Using a Dictionary

Put these words into alphabetical order.

Read each word and decide whether it is spelt correctly. If you think it is not, write a different spelling underneath. Then find the word in the dictionary and tick the correct spelling.

Look up each word in the dictionary. Write the meaning on the lines and draw a picture in the box.

fern _____

llama _____

<ai>
<ay>
<a_e>

Look at the pictures and write the words underneath.

  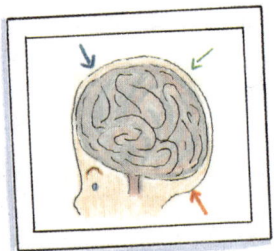

stay
tail
mail
male
spray
shape

crayon
praying
mainly
layer
escape
pancake

birthday
yesterday
waiting
ailing
animate
decade

Look up each word in the dictionary and read its definition. Write the page number in the snail.

snail   male   date
weigh   layer   pancake

Put these words into alphabetical order.

dragon phoenix yeti   china cheese chops   string struck street

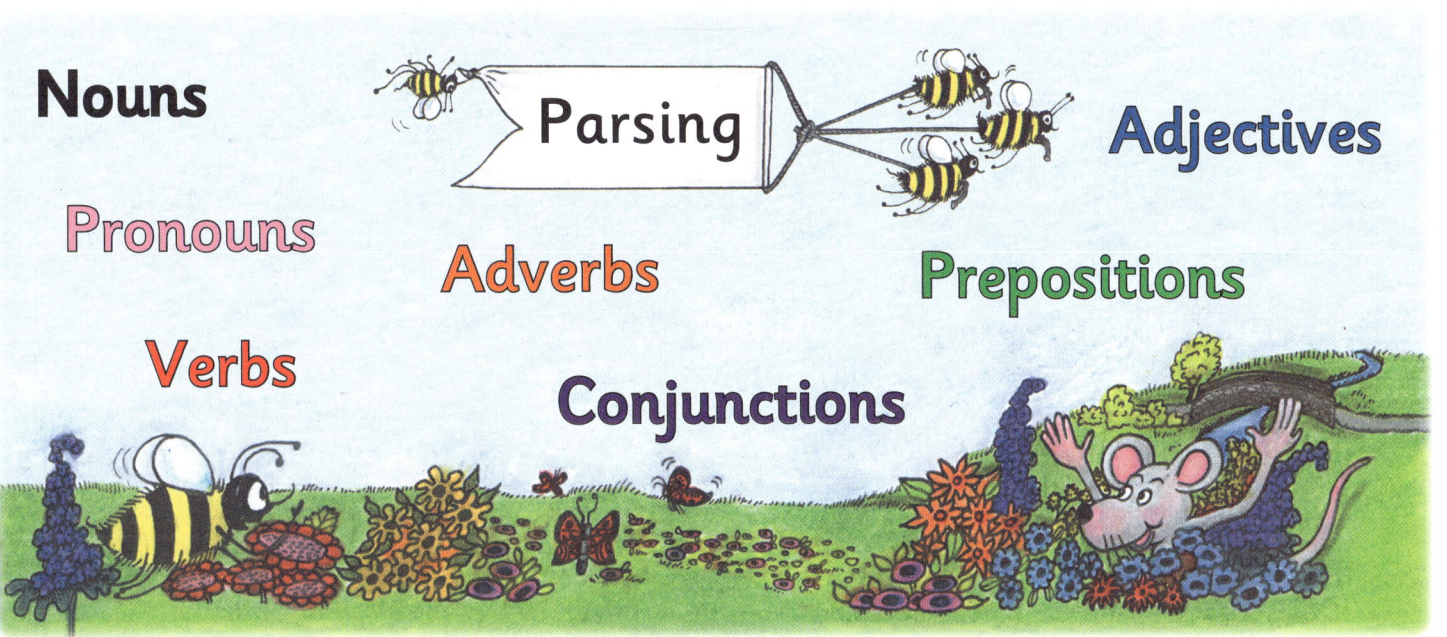

Identify as many of the different parts of speech as you can and underline them in the correct colours.

Snake's Surprise

Inky skipped happily down the dusty road and over a low bridge. She saw her friend Bee in the big meadow. Bee buzzed busily while she flew from flower to flower. Inky called, "Bee," loudly and waved, so her friend zoomed quickly across the meadow.

They walked into the forest and saw Snake. He slithered slowly among the trees towards his friends. They watched as he put a square box carefully on the bumpy ground.

"Is it a present for Inky?" Bee asked excitedly.

"I have yummy cakes for tea because it is a special day," hissed Snake.

"A special day?" repeated Bee and Inky.

"I played my drum and passed my exam. I am a good drummer!" exclaimed Snake with a big grin.

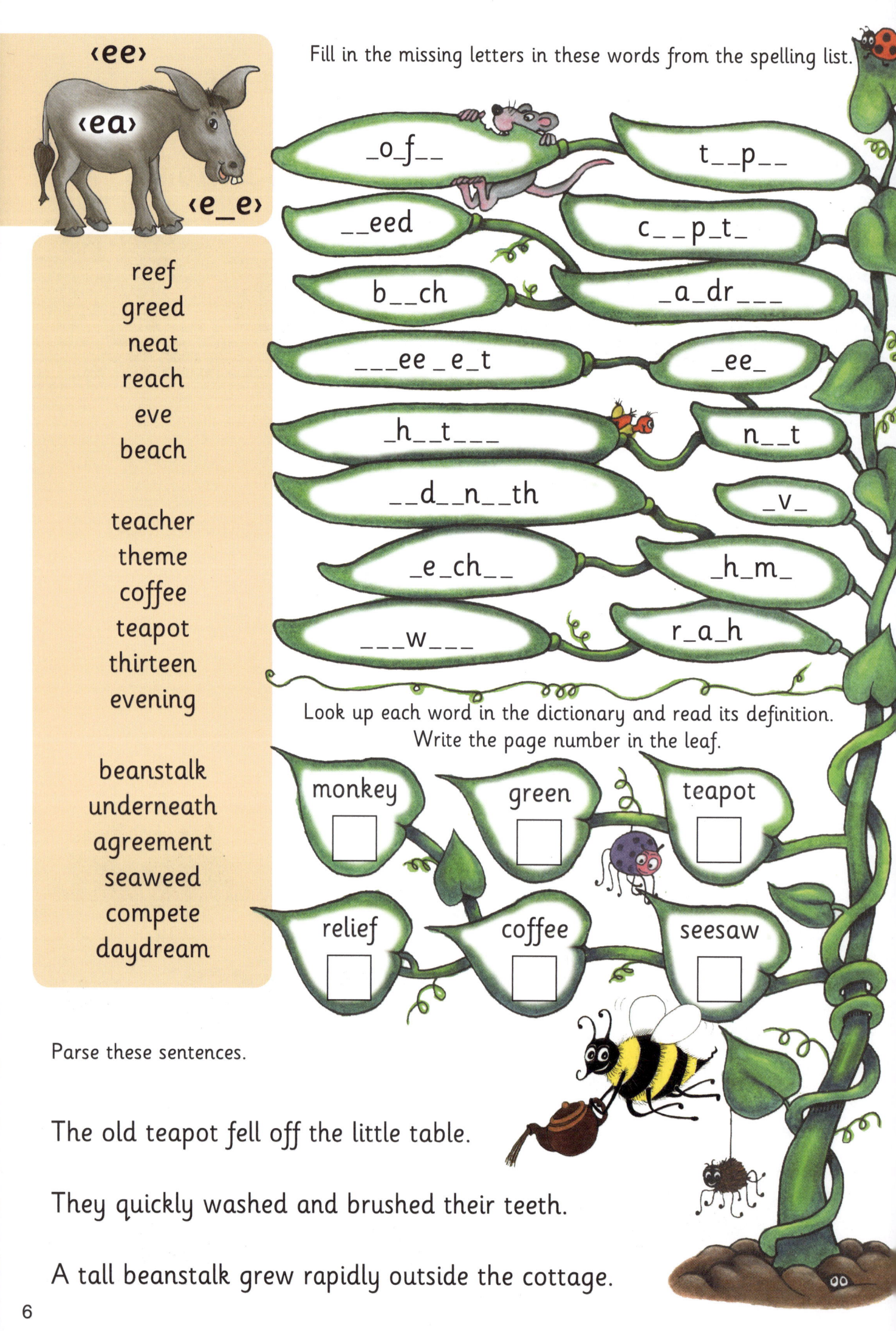

Verbs

Simple Tenses

Write these verbs in the simple past tense.

to hum _____

to play _____

to cook _____

to nod _____

to like _____

to tap _____

In each sentence, underline the verb in red. Then decide if the sentence is in the past, present or future, and put a tick in the right column. Colour the bees when you have finished.

	Past	Present	Future
I <u>shall cook</u> dinner tomorrow.			✓
We played at Sam's house.			
He rides his bike in the park.			
Sally eats her lunch hungrily.			
She will run in the race on Saturday.			
He patted his friend's dog.			
You climb up the tree.			
They will go to the museum next week.			
At the concert I sang a song.			
Tonight we shall look at the stars.			
I am good at football.			
Last week we painted animals in art.			

Past
Point backwards over your shoulder with your thumb.

Present
Point towards the floor with the palm of your hand.

Future
Point to the front.

Find the words from the spelling list. Which one is missing?

life
high
flies
spying
dive
tied

dryer
tried
alright
firework
alive
delight

describe
asylum
lightning
frightening
butterfly
pantomime

Look up each word in the dictionary and read its definition. Write the page number in the die.

Parse these sentences.

Granny makes a tasty pie.

The brave knight swiftly rescued the princess.

The black and white magpie flies in the blue sky.

8

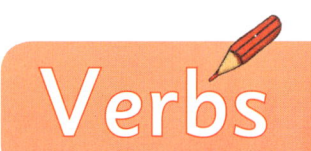

Simple Tenses

Verbs

Write the simple present tense of each verb in the third person singular.

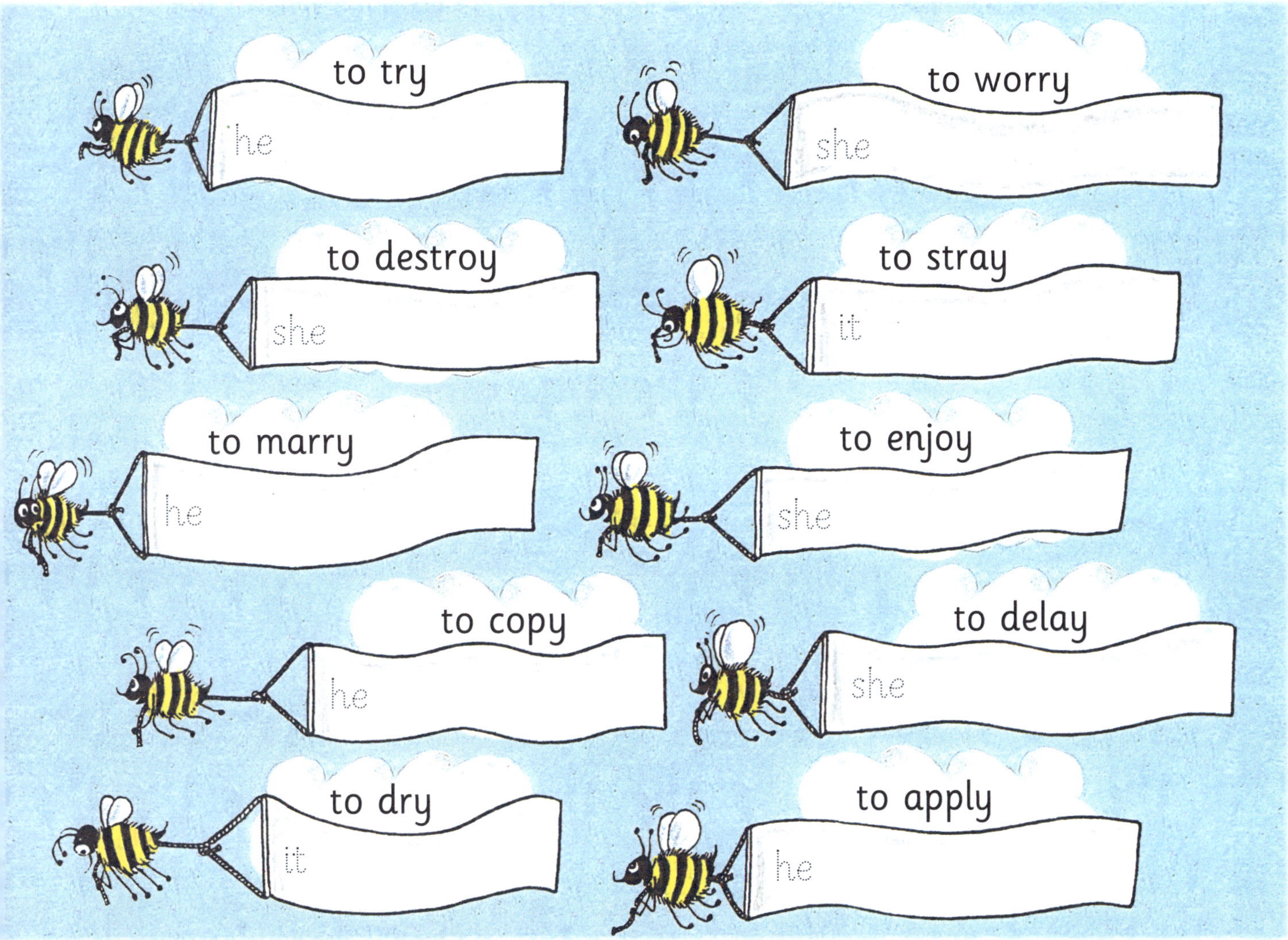

to try — he

to worry — she

to destroy — she

to stray — it

to marry — he

to enjoy — she

to copy — he

to delay — she

to dry — it

to apply — he

Choose one of the verbs and conjugate it.

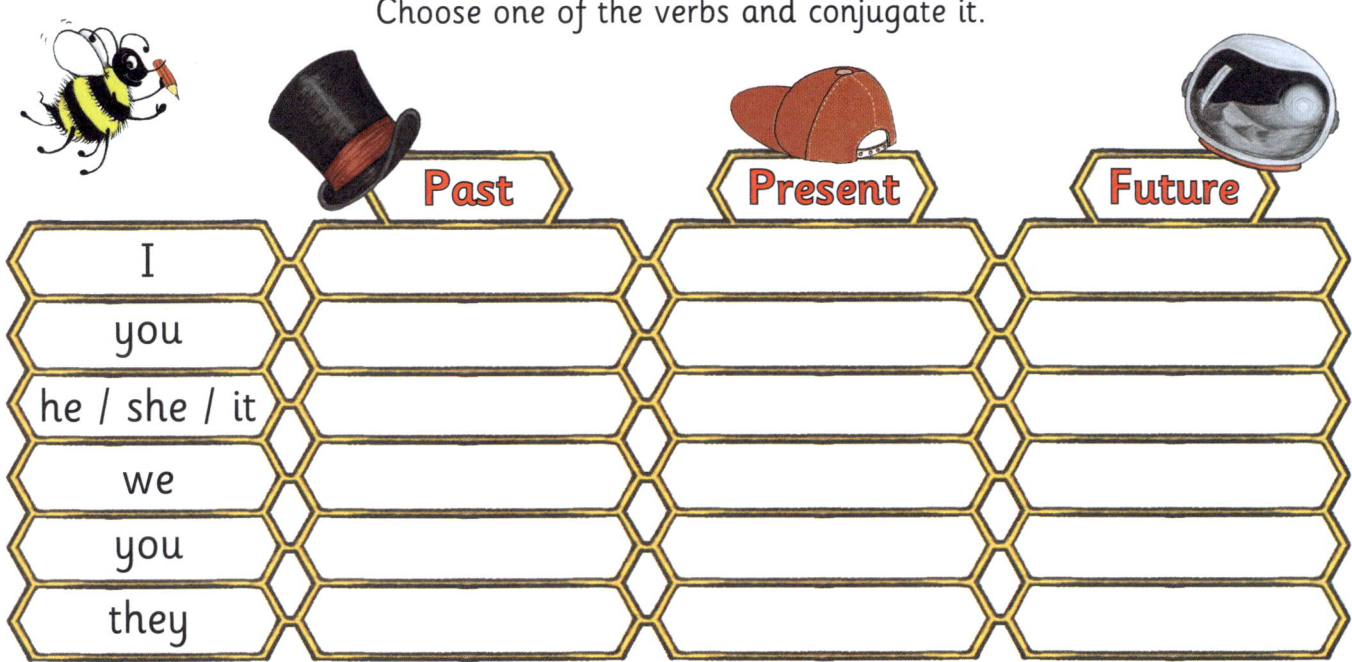

	Past	Present	Future
I			
you			
he / she / it			
we			
you			
they			

⟨oa⟩ ⟨ow⟩ ⟨o_e⟩

float
joke
croak
elbow
owner
alone

follow
explode
homework
moaning
shadow
slowest

rainbow
approach
tightrope
cockroach
hormone
envelope

Which words in the spelling list match these descriptions?

1. _____ (something funny)
2. _____ (on your own)
3. _____ (the opposite of 'sink')
4. _____ (an arm joint)
5. _____ (an insect)
6. _____ (the opposite of 'quickest')
7. _____ (to get nearer)
8. _____ (to sound like a frog)
9. _____ (it has lots of colours)
10. _____ (to burst into little pieces)

Look up each word in the dictionary and read its definition.
Write the page number in the oak leaf.

Parse these sentences.

She will grow yellow primroses.

The snow fell thickly on the road.

The fearless acrobat walked slowly across the tightrope.

Verbs

'to be'

Conjugate the verb 'to be' in the past, present and future.

Past	Present	Future
I was	I am	I shall be

In each sentence, underline the verb 'to be' in red. Then decide whether the sentence is in the past, present or future.

It <u>was</u> cold last night. **past**

We were happy.

She is very intelligent.

They will be at the concert.

You were very good at Grandma's house.

The cat is tabby and white.

I was sad when the holidays ended.

I am in the school play.

We shall be in town at the weekend.

⟨ue⟩ ⟨ew⟩

⟨u_e⟩

Put the words in the spelling list into the crossword.

1. cue
2. flute
3. amuse
4. statue
5. threw
6. fewer

7. bluebell
8. venue
9. pollute
10. volume
11. newt
12. fortune

13. Yuletide
14. avenue
15. attitude
16. costume
17. absolute
18. screwdriver

Look up each word in the dictionary and read its definition. Write the page number in the tube.

Parse these sentences.

The tasty stew cooked slowly.

He argued angrily with his little sister.

My dad reads his daily newspaper while he is on the train.

Syllables

Identify and underline the vowel sounds in these words. Then split the words into syllables with a line.

bluebell farmyard playtime hairbrush

jigsaw weekend breakfast seaweed

Do the same again with these words, which have prefixes and suffixes.

unkind dislike thankful disagree

unless undo prefix slowly

Identify the vowel sounds in these words. If a word has one vowel sound, decide whether the vowel is short or long, and put ‹◡› over a short vowel and ‹—› or ‹—•› over a long vowel. If a word has more than one vowel sound, underline the vowels and split the syllables as before.

măn lēek footstep badly skip

goalkeeper hopeful lighthouse

hop clockwise rain teacher

clap earthworm play toilet

swim sleeveless boat uneventful run

unimportant yesterday handkerchief

REMEMBER 'Monosyllabic' words cannot be split into more than one syllable because they only have one vowel sound.

‹e_e›

gene
these
recede
delete
impede
scheme

concede
stampede
complete
extreme
athlete
concrete

supreme
intervene
phoneme
Chinese
obsolete
centipede

Find the words from the spelling list. Which one is missing?

a	t	i	c	e	n	t	i	p	e	d	e	y	b
d	e	l	e	t	e	v	u	r	e	c	e	d	e
i	s	g	i	n	t	e	r	v	e	n	e	a	w
k	c	o	n	c	r	e	t	e	o	z	e	n	e
a	n	g	e	t	e	l	s	c	h	e	m	e	r
c	o	m	p	l	e	t	e	r	t	h	e	s	e
t	g	b	j	p	h	o	n	e	m	e	f	s	t
a	t	h	l	e	t	e	j	q	u	e	d	e	v
g	l	s	s	t	a	m	p	e	d	e	g	h	v
w	o	b	s	o	l	e	t	e	j	e	m	e	u
g	e	n	e	z	s	u	p	r	e	m	e	a	i
p	r	m	u	c	o	n	c	e	d	e	p	u	y
s	q	u	e	s	e	l	i	m	p	e	d	e	z
t	h	e	x	t	r	e	m	e	c	h	a	i	x

Look up each word in the dictionary and read its definition. Write the page number in the theme park.

theme   delete   scheme

evening   concrete   athlete

Split these words into syllables. For words of one syllable add the long or short vowel symbol.

concrete   these   athlete   extreme   intervene

Parse these sentences.

The athletes will compete in the morning.

I accidentally deleted my work on the computer.

Present Participle

Colour the pictures when you've finished.

Add ‹-ing› to these verbs to make the present participle.

walk + ing

boil _____
deliver _____
inject _____
perform _____
sprout _____

wipe + ing

amuse _____
describe _____
serve _____
exercise _____
wipe _____

hop + p + ing

admit _____
shop _____
grin _____
knit _____
stop _____

cry + ing

carry _____
dry _____
hurry _____
stay _____
tidy _____

die + y + ing

lie _____   tie _____

Write the present participle of these verbs.

fly _____   grab _____   remind _____
measure _____   juggle _____   plan _____
frighten _____   tie _____   irritate _____

‹n›

anger
skunk
tanker
junk
trunk
sunken

anchor
blanket
finger
hunger
angler
extinct

stinking
handkerchief
anguish
distinctive
defunct
singular

Read the word and draw a picture to illustrate it.

skunk	anchor
angler	monk
finger	tanker

Look up each word in the dictionary and read its definition. Write the page number in the blanket.

bank   wink   angler
extinct   junk   linger

Split these words into syllables. For words of one syllable add the long or short vowel symbol.

skunk   blanket   junk   tanker   handkerchief

Parse these sentences.

The Chinese junk anchored safely in the bay.

The black and white skunk ran quickly into the wood.

Present Continuous

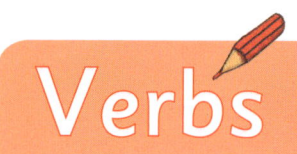

Conjugate the verb 'to be' in simple present tense.

I _____   you _____   he / she / it _____

we _____   you _____   they _____

In each sentence, underline the verb in red and choose the correct tense.

She is cooking spaghetti for dinner.
She cooks spaghetti for dinner.

- simple present
- present continuous

We jog around the park.
We are jogging around the park.

- simple present
- present continuous

The baby is crawling across the floor.
The baby crawls across the floor.

- simple present
- present continuous

They are screaming on the roller coaster.
They scream on the roller coaster.

- simple present
- present continuous

Rewrite these sentences in the present continuous tense.

Colour the pictures when you've finished.

I draw a picture in my sketchbook.

_____

They play football in the park.

_____

The little dog yaps loudly.

_____

We jump on the trampoline.

_____

‹ci› ‹ce› ‹cy›

Put the words in the spelling list into the crossword.

1	race
2	space
3	since
4	twice
5	cancel
6	princess
7	office
8	palace
9	voice
10	silence
11	bounce
12	incident
13	accident
14	medicine
15	cereal
16	vacancy
17	advance
18	cinnamon

Look up each word in the dictionary and read its definition. Write the page number in the bouncy ball.

acid   police   voice   celery   twice   balance

Split these words into syllables. For words of one syllable add the long or short vowel symbol.

race   cancel   princess   silence   vacancy

Parse these sentences.

Sam bounced the ball high into the air.

They cancelled the race because it was icy.

Past Continuous
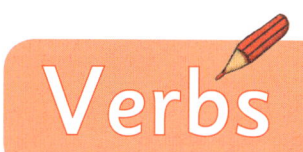

Conjugate the verb 'to be' in the simple past tense.

I _____   you _____   he / she / it _____

we _____   you _____   they _____

Underline the verbs in these sentences in red and the pronouns in pink. Then rewrite each sentence in the past continuous tense.

She skips in the park.
_____

I milk the cows in the morning.
_____

We jump over the waves at the beach.
_____

They rake up the leaves on the lawn.
_____

You help at the swimming club.
_____

He dusts the ornaments.
_____

Join each sentence to the correct tense.

They were playing in the park. 🌸
They play in the park. 🌸
They are playing in the park. 🌸
They played in the park. 🌸

🌸 simple present
🌸 simple past
🌸 present continuous
🌸 past continuous

19

 # Places

Proper Nouns
Touch your forehead with your index and middle fingers.

Write the names of three famous places, then illustrate each one.

1. _____   2. _____   3. _____

Write the names of ten countries.

_____ _____ _____ _____ _____

_____ _____ _____ _____ _____

Write the names of the seven continents.

_____ _____ _____ _____

_____ _____ _____

Find all of the proper nouns in the postcard and make sure they start with a capital letter.

Dear aunty pam and uncle horace,
   We are having a lovely time on holiday in summershire. We have visited the beautiful village of sheldown and the town of brington. Yesterday we went to the happywood hills home for horses. Dan sponsored a donkey called merry.
   Lots of love from,
   suzie, will, dan and ruby

mr and mrs h smith,
8 hill road,
frickleton,
suffolk,
england, europe, earth

‹tch›

Which words in the spelling list match these descriptions?

1. _____ (a room for cooking)
2. _____ (a very simple drawing)
3. _____ (a pet rabbit lives here)
4. _____ (it carries injured people)
5. _____ (to grab away)
6. _____ (a man who sells meat)
7. _____ (very miserable or ill)
8. _____ (it is used to light a fire)
9. _____ (a cold, red sauce)
10. _____ (it turns a light on and off)

itch
catch
fetch
witch
match
hutch

kitchen
snatch
butcher
switch
sketch
crutches

watching
stretcher
ketchup
wretched
scratching
stretching

Look up each word in the dictionary and read its definition.
Write the page number in the watch.

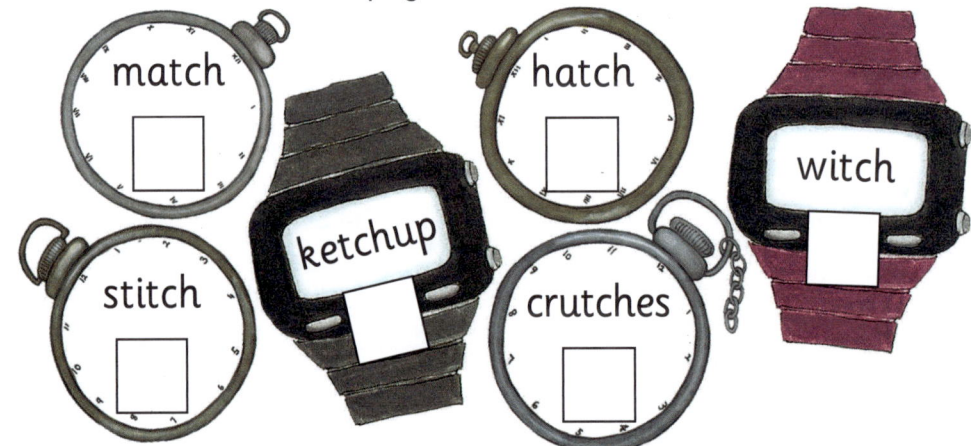

Parse the sentences and write over the dotted letters.

The small boy quickly put his books in his satchel.

I watched the quiet fisherman on the riverbank.

tch tch
tch tch tch
tch
tch tch

Proper Adjectives

REMEMBER Proper adjectives need a capital letter at the beginning.

Action

Touch the side of your temple with your fist.

Complete each sentence by writing the correct proper adjective in the gap.

Kangaroos are _____ animals.
(Australia)

I watched the _____ dancers.
(Spain)

This is the _____ flag.
(Japan)

The Union Jack is the _____ flag.
(Britain)

We went to the _____ burger bar.
(America)

Mounties are _____ police officers.
(Canada)

This is a _____ book.
(France)

There is a _____ junk in the port.
(China)

My granny likes _____ tea.
(India)

‹dge›

Add ‹dge› to complete each word and then draw a picture.

bri____

ba____

sle____

ba____r

he____hog

bu____rigar

edge
judge
sledge
badge
badger
bridge

gadget
budge
fidget
ledge
hedgerow
hedgehog

knowledge
begrudge
porridge
budgerigar
drawbridge
partridge

Look up each word in the dictionary and read its definition. Write the page number in the hedgehog.

drawbridge
budge
fidget
hedgehog
smudge
porridge

Write over the dotted letters.

dge dge dge dge dge dge dge

Parse these sentences.

We are waiting eagerly for the judge.

The badger quickly disappeared through the hedge.

Syllables

Identify and underline the vowel sounds in these words then split the words into syllables with a line. Write out the syllables in the logs beneath.

lad/der	kitten	cracker
lad der		
jogging	cricket	pepper

bramble	ankle	jungle
simple	uncle	thimble

pebble	pickle	dazzle
assemble	sunsaddle	unbuckle

⟨le⟩

Put the words in the spelling list into alphabetical order.

1. _____   10. _____
2. _____   11. _____
3. _____   12. _____
4. _____   13. _____
5. _____   14. _____
6. _____   15. _____
7. _____   16. _____
8. _____   17. _____
9. _____   18. _____

simple
eagle
beetle
handle
puzzle
angle

jungle
horrible
terrible
knuckle
disable
obstacle

formidable
improbable
impossible
rectangle
believable
vehicle

Look up each word in the dictionary and read its definition. Write the page number in the puzzle piece.

puzzle ☐   jungle ☐   vehicle ☐
battle ☐   saddle ☐   juggle ☐

Split these words into syllables.

eagle   tickle   handle   saddle   rectangle

Parse these sentences.

The Scottish eagle floated lazily on the breeze.

The tiny black beetles scuttle quickly under the rotten log.

‹qu›

Which words in the spelling list match these descriptions?

1. _____ (the same value as)
2. _____ (to sound like a mouse)
3. _____ (a big dinner)
4. _____ (to ask)
5. _____ (a furry-tailed animal)
6. _____ (where fish are kept)
7. _____ (a line around the world)
8. _____ (to shake or tremble)
9. _____ (an argument)
10. _____ (the tools for a job)

quiver
equal
request
quote
liquid
squeak

quite
quarrel
squeeze
squirrel
squash
aquatic

conquest
banquet
aquarium
equipment
eloquent
equator

Look up each word in the dictionary and read its definition. Write the page number in the square.

Split these words into syllables. For words of one syllable add the long or short vowel symbol.

request   squeak   squeeze   frequent   equipment

Parse these sentences.

I bought a new aquarium for my goldfish.

The red squirrel quivered and squeaked at the smelly skunk.

Paragraphs

Write over each heading.
Then write a paragraph about that topic underneath.

All About Me

Me and My Family

Where I Live

My Hobbies

easy
busy
nose
result
prison
dismal

cosmic
positive
misery
present
president
raspberry

phase
invisible
business
inquisitive
preposition
enthusiastic

Find the words from the spelling list. Which one is missing?

s	p	r	e	p	o	s	i	t	i	o	n	e	r
c	o	s	m	i	c	c	h	e	a	s	y	l	l
r	i	p	h	a	s	e	a	t	n	o	s	e	d
i	n	v	i	s	i	b	l	e	m	o	r	d	y
c	b	u	s	y	m	p	o	s	i	t	i	v	e
e	s	s	u	p	r	e	s	e	n	t	i	n	t
p	r	o	v	a	b	u	s	i	n	e	s	s	t
p	r	e	s	i	d	e	n	t	e	r	m	i	t
s	h	r	a	s	p	b	e	r	r	y	i	g	h
d	i	s	m	a	l	n	t	a	b	l	i	m	o
f	r	e	s	u	l	t	q	u	o	c	k	o	u
w	a	v	i	x	p	r	i	s	o	n	a	i	d
o	z	i	n	q	u	i	s	i	t	i	v	e	j
e	n	t	h	u	s	i	a	s	t	i	c	a	l

Look up each word in the dictionary and read its definition. Write the page number in the daisy.

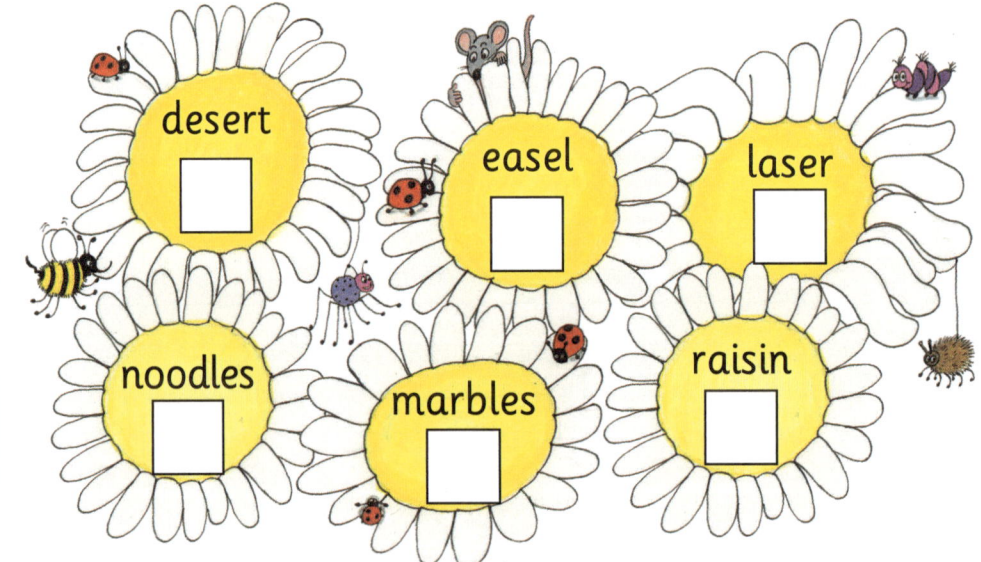

desert   easel   laser   noodles   marbles   raisin

Split these words into syllables. For words of one syllable add the long or short vowel symbol.

dismal   nose   clumsy   drowsy   raspberry

Parse these sentences.

I carefully cut the paper with my sharp scissors.

He quickly ate the English raspberries and cream for dessert.

"Speech Marks"

Fill in the missing punctuation marks.

 ☐ The fireworks are brilliant ☐☐ said Bill ☐

Write out the words in the speech bubbles as sentences.

Sam  I feel sick.

_____
_____

I don't want to go. **Lily**

_____
_____

Megan  I've fallen over and hurt my knee.

_____
_____

The roller coaster was very scary.  **Seth**

_____
_____

Anna  I'm going to Granny's for supper tomorrow.

_____
_____

REMEMBER Explain who is speaking and add in the correct punctuation.

Put the words in the spelling list into alphabetical order.

1. _____   10. _____
2. _____   11. _____
3. _____   12. _____
4. _____   13. _____
5. _____   14. _____
6. _____   15. _____
7. _____   16. _____
8. _____   17. _____
9. _____   18. _____

ooze
sneeze
cheese
choose
freeze
wheeze

breeze
noise
browse
bronze
pause
cause

disease
bruise
applause
appraise
turquoise
mayonnaise

Look up each word in the dictionary and read its definition. Write the page number in the cheese.

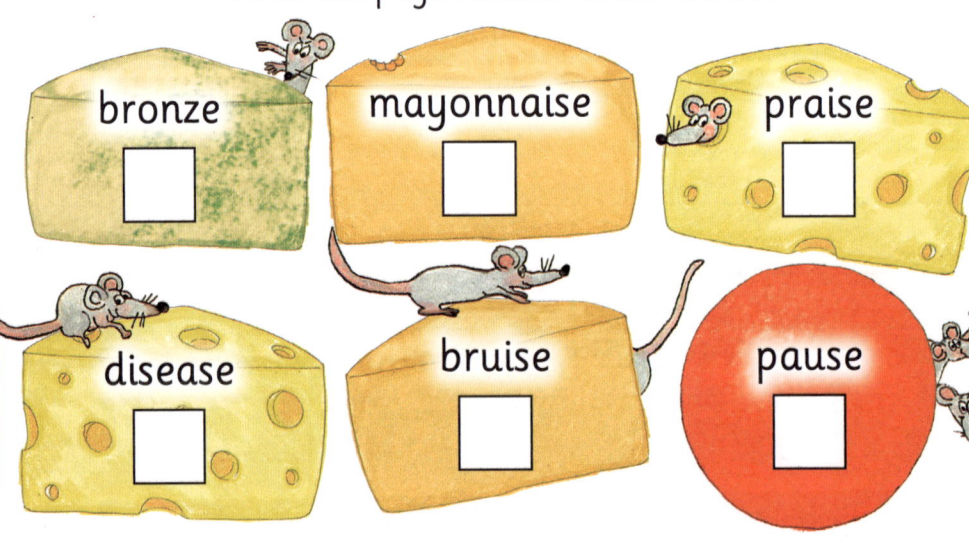

bronze   mayonnaise   praise
disease   bruise   pause

Split these words into syllables. For words of one syllable add the long or short vowel symbol.

wheeze   appraise   turquoise   please   mayonnaise

Parse these sentences.

I sneeze and wheeze in the winter.

The old American jeep reversed noisily outside our house.

32

"Speech Marks"

What do you think the two boys are saying? Write their words in the speech bubbles.

Now write out the conversation as sentences.

‹-less›

Fill in the missing letters in these words from the spelling list.

u_e____   b_t_____
p_t_____   t_m_____
___m____   w__th____
_ea_____   __aw____
c_____   h_l_____
__m____   _r__th____
p__n____   _r_c_____
__i__t____   __d____

useless
helpless
endless
painless
aimless
flawless

worthless
fearless
timeless
harmless
speechless
bottomless

priceless
careless
pitiless
breathless
flightless
weightless

Look up each word in the dictionary and read its definition. Write the page number in the priceless vase.

useless   careless   aimless
endless   breathless   helpless

Split these words into syllables.

sleeveless   priceless   cloudless   speechless   effortless

Parse these sentences.

The dull story seemed endless.

The extinct dodo was a flightless bird.

Future Continuous

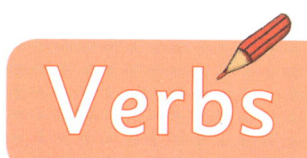

Conjugate the sentence in the future continuous.

I paint a picture.

I <u>shall be painting a picture.</u>
You _____
He / She / It _____
We _____
You _____
They _____

In each sentence, find the verb and underline it in red.

I <u style="color:red">shall be grinning</u> if I win.

He will be competing in the hopping race.

You will be dancing in the summer show.

She will be walking a long way on her trip.

They will be composing a song for the concert.

You will be digging the vegetable patch.

We shall be joining the other class today.

Choose the correct tense for each sentence.

They were playing cards. — simple past

I shall play cards. — simple present

He plays cards. — simple future

You will be playing cards. — past continuous

We played cards. — present continuous

She is playing cards. — future continuous

35

Make new words by adding the suffix ‹-able›.
Write the new words on the lines.

break _____
wash _____
value _____
size _____
enjoy _____
rely _____
suit _____
comfort _____
adore _____
hug _____
desire _____
pity _____

avoidable
profitable
available
portable
adaptable
dependable

breakable
usable
lovable
irritable
enjoyable
debatable

changeable
disposable
desirable
miserable
variable
noticeable

Look up each word in the dictionary and read its definition.
Write the page number in the comfortable cushion.

Split these words into syllables.

enjoyable   lovable   huggable   reliable   usable

Parse these sentences.

The dirty shirt is washable.

The sofa was old but comfortable.

Suffixes

Use both suffixes with each fish to make pairs of adjectives with opposite meanings. Then use each adjective in a sentence.

1. powerful
   powerless

2.

3.

4.

5.

6.

⟨a⟩

crazy
taste
basic
baby
haste
maple

inhaler
pastry
acorn
stable
vacant
chamber

plague
chaotic
stranger
adjacent
newspaper
conversation

Read each word and draw a picture for it in the box.

cradle

baby

acorn

lady

stable

raven

Look up each word in the dictionary and read its definition. Write the page number in the labelled parcel.

table   apron   gravy

lazy   famous   raven

Split these words into syllables.

basic   lazy   vacant   newspaper   conversation

Parse these sentences.

The beautiful lady ate a tasty pastry.

The lazy alien is lying in the lunar crater.

38

Contractions

REMEMBER We only use contractions when writing speech or a friendly note.

Write each pair of words as a contraction by joining them together and replacing ‹wi› or ‹sha› with an apostrophe.

I shall _____   you will _____
he will _____   she will _____
it will _____   we shall _____
you will _____   they will _____

In each sentence, write out the contraction in full as two words and with no letters missing.

She'll be competing in the cross-country race.

_____

They'll be trying to climb the mountain this year.

_____

You'll be playing in the football team next week.

_____

Rewrite each sentence, using contractions.

We shall be watching the fireworks tonight.

_____

He will be collecting his son from school later.

_____

I'll you'll she'll we'll they'll

⟨e⟩

evil
email
secret
legal
fever
regal

female
prefect
recent
media
create
medium

frequent
adhesive
medieval
chameleon
immediate
prehistoric

Put the words in the spelling list into alphabetical order.

1. _____ 10. _____
2. _____ 11. _____
3. _____ 12. _____
4. _____ 13. _____
5. _____ 14. _____
6. _____ 15. _____
7. _____ 16. _____
8. _____ 17. _____
9. _____ 18. _____

Look up each word in the dictionary and read its definition.
Write the page number in the prefect badge.

create   apostrophe   arena

prefix   equal   senior

Split these words into syllables.

reflex   email   female   genius   frequent

Parse these sentences.

She will be visiting her grandparents.

An emu is a large Australian bird.

Comparatives and Superlatives

In each sentence, find the adjective and underline it in blue. Then rewrite the sentence, first using the comparative, and then using the superlative.

That mouse is <u>small</u>.

_____

_____

The monster had a loud voice.

_____

_____

He is a tall man.

_____

_____

This is a wise owl.

_____

_____

Which clown was funny?

_____

_____

Those elephants are grey.

_____

_____

⟨i⟩

Find the words from the spelling list.
Which one is missing?

p	b	o	b	e	h	i	n	d	m	p	l	e	s
o	i	c	y	k	n	u	c	c	h	i	l	d	b
i	d	e	a	o	x	g	i	g	a	n	t	i	c
u	s	h	i	b	e	r	n	a	t	e	a	c	k
f	w	e	a	t	h	o	r	i	z	o	n	a	y
c	h	u	e	w	d	s	p	h	i	a	l	i	n
g	m	i	c	r	o	p	h	o	n	e	a	j	t
q	u	x	m	d	i	a	g	o	n	a	l	g	h
o	p	i	r	a	t	e	v	a	i	s	t	e	r
a	r	g	u	s	b	q	u	i	e	t	h	o	n
k	e	n	g	d	i	a	r	y	q	u	o	r	x
z	r	a	s	s	w	i	l	d	h	i	l	s	h
a	g	e	p	h	o	r	i	c	o	n	a	l	z
s	p	i	d	e	r	g	y	d	i	e	t	i	n

icy
icon
diet
child
idea
wild

behind
spider
pirate
diary
Viking
horizon

phial
quiet
gigantic
diagonal
microphone
hibernate

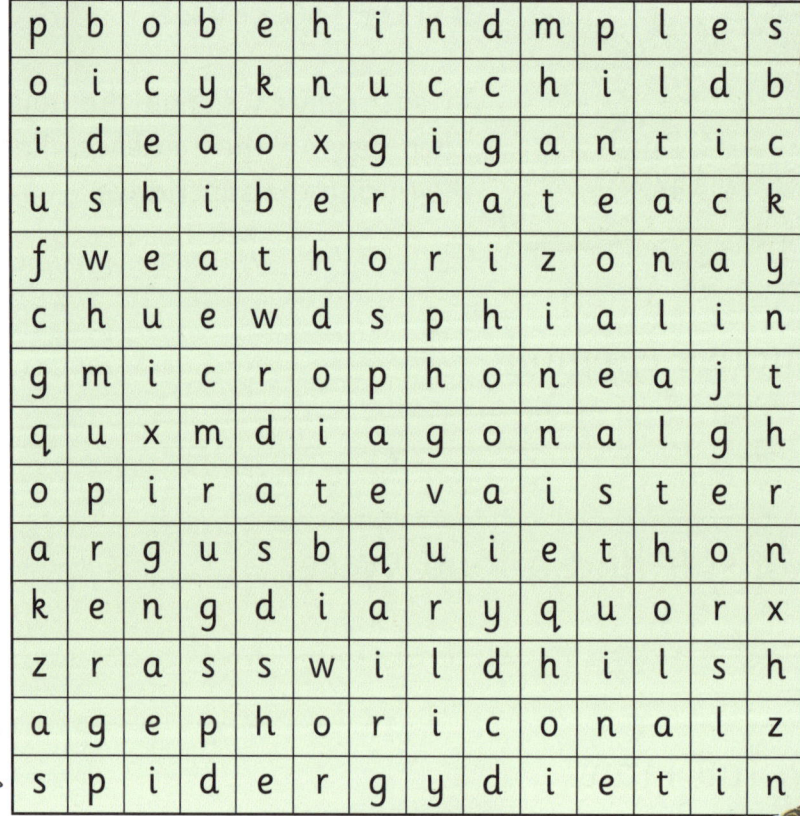

Look up each word in the dictionary and read its definition.
Write the page number in the diary.

final   giant   violin   climb   horizon   pirate

Split these words into syllables. For words of one syllable add the long or short vowel symbol.

final   find   tiger   hijack   microwave

Parse these sentences.

The fiercest African lion was roaring loudly.

Hedgehogs hibernate in winter.

Adverbs Made by Adding ‹-ly› to Adjectives

Make these adjectives into adverbs.

Adjectives	heavy	selfish	quiet	angry	bad
Adverbs					

Make each adjective, underlined in blue, into an adverb and complete the sentence.

The boy had a **quick** snack. He ate his snack _____.

He had a **serious** injury. He injured himself _____.

I am a **careful** driver. I drive _____.

It is a **safe** place to cross. You can cross _____.

She was a **happy** child. The child lived _____.

It was an **easy** test to pass. I passed the test _____.

Here are some adverbs made from adjectives. Choose three and write a sentence for each.

1. _____

2. _____

3. _____

⟨o⟩

Put the words in the spelling list into the crossword.

1	open
2	oval
3	only
4	poem
5	total
6	clover
7	mosaic
8	cocoa
9	mobile
10	Roman
11	pronoun
12	moment
13	ogre
14	anchovy
15	overboard
16	vocabulary
17	macaroni
18	steamroller

Look up each word in the dictionary and read its definition. Write the page number in the coconut.

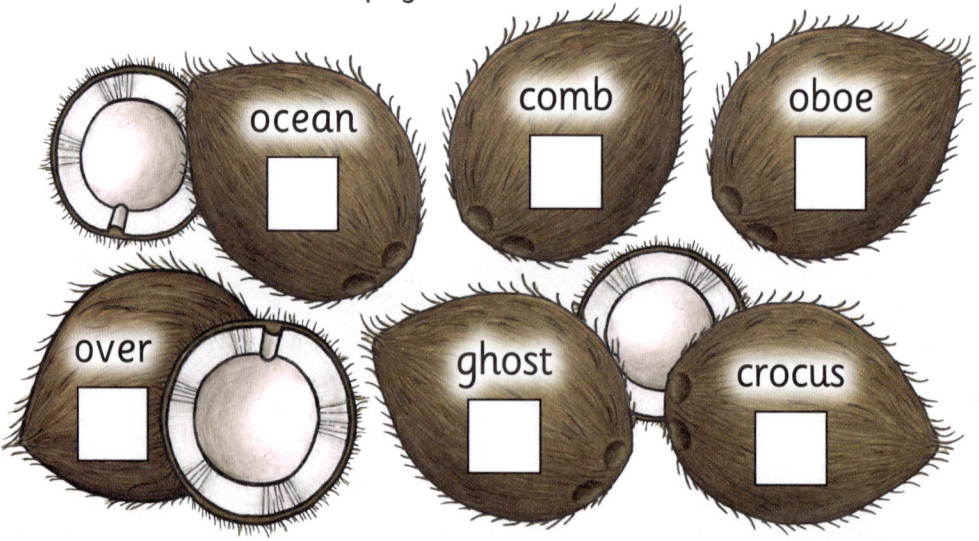

Split these words into syllables.

robot   okay   overboard   coconut   October

Parse these sentences.

They uncovered a Roman mosaic in the villa.

The oboe is a musical instrument.

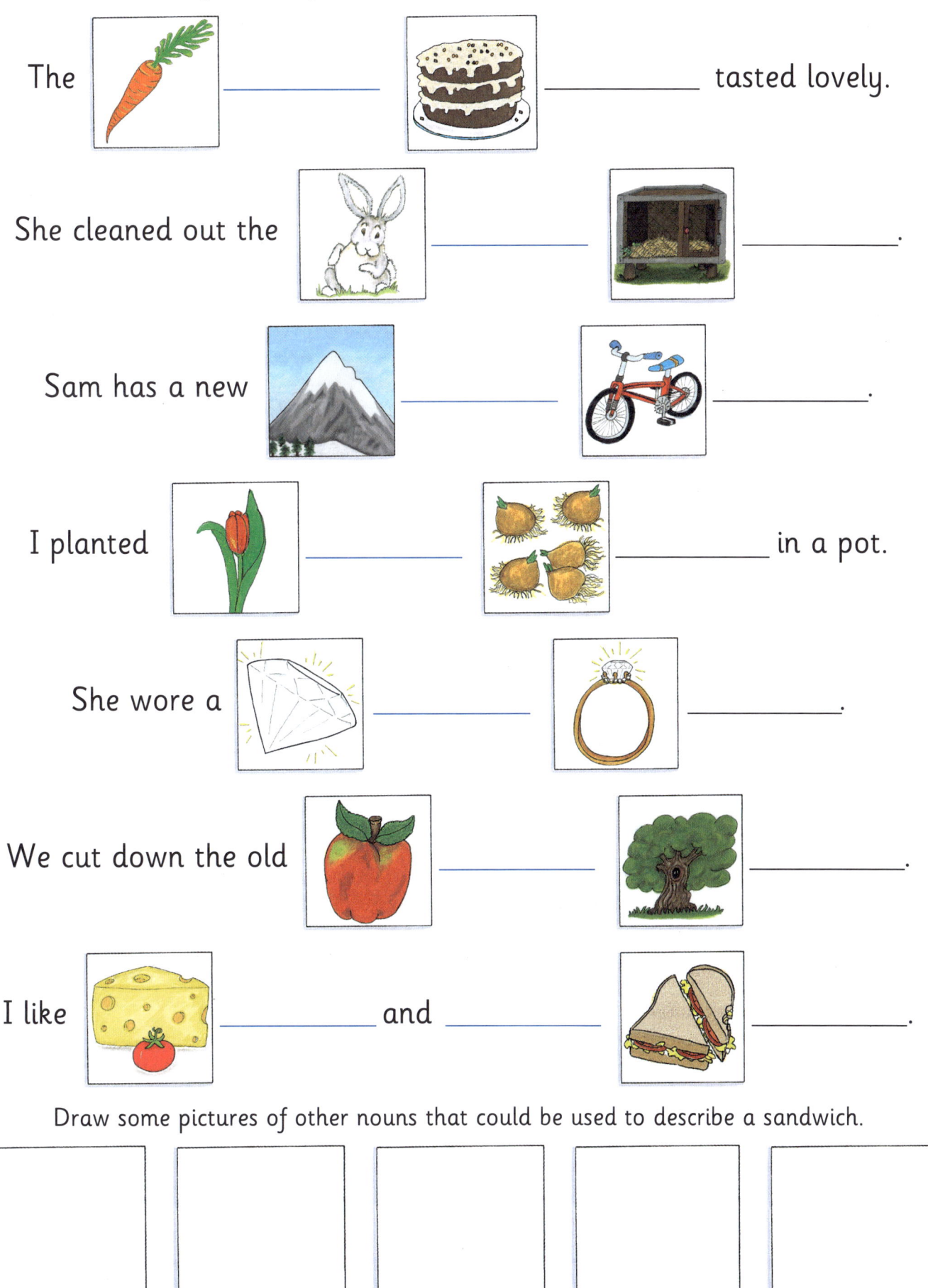

⟨-os⟩ ⟨-o⟩ ⟨-oes⟩

Make each word plural by adding ‹-es›.
Then count the dots and draw the correct number of pictures.

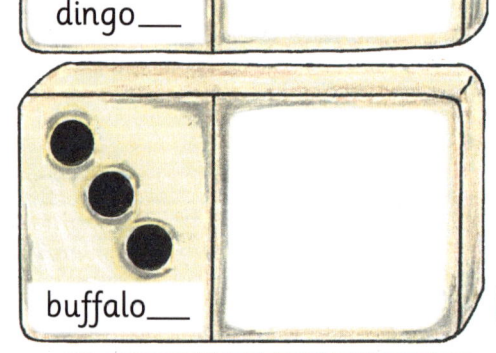

dingo__

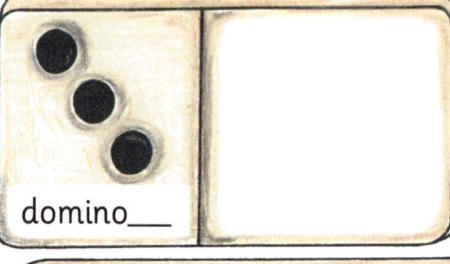

domino__

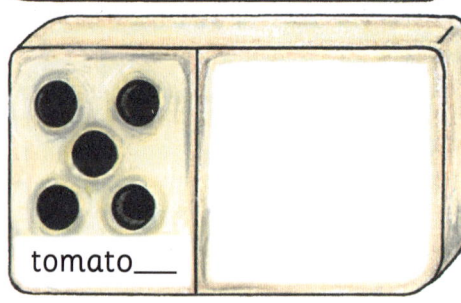

buffalo__

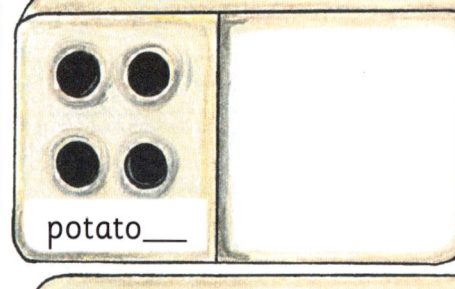

potato__

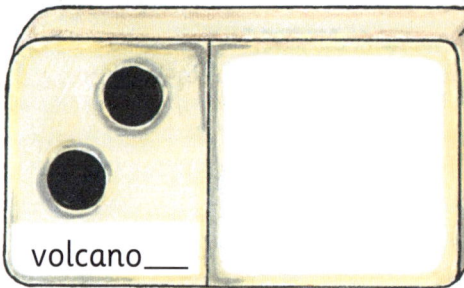

tomato__   volcano__

ago
hero
dodo
zero
echo
hello

mango
pianos
radios
videos
tornado
volcano

flamingo
memento
mosquito
torpedoes
tomatoes
potatoes

Look up each word in the dictionary and read its definition.
Write the page number in the potato.

indigo   motto   bingo

cargo   armadillo   studio

Split these words into syllables.

disco   photo   mango   torpedo   mosquito

Parse these sentences.

She will be playing a piano concerto.

The volcano exploded violently.

Adjectives Made by Adding ‹-y› to Nouns

Make these nouns into adjectives.

Nouns	dust	spice	mud	noise	hair	spot
Adjectives						

Make each noun, underlined in black, into an adjective and complete the sentence.

The old bike had lots of <u>rust</u>. It was a _____ bike.

Wish on the star for <u>luck</u>. It is a _____ star.

They sat in the <u>shade</u> of the tree. It was a _____ tree.

We squeezed <u>juice</u> from the lemons. The lemons were _____.

My bedroom is in a <u>mess</u>. My bedroom is _____.

There are many <u>clouds</u> in the sky. The sky is _____.

Here are some adjectives made from nouns. Choose three and write a sentence for each.

foggy   greedy   lumpy   rosy   dirty
hilly   thorny   wealthy   windy
fluffy

1. _____

2. _____

3. _____

 ⟨u⟩

Which words in the spelling list match these descriptions?

1. _____ (a list of food for serving)
2. _____ (all the stars and planets)
3. _____ (a type of fish)
4. _____ (a song for two singers)
5. _____ (an electronic machine)
6. _____ (to say something)
7. _____ (a flightless bird)
8. _____ (strange or unfamiliar)
9. _____ (a bike with one wheel)
10. _____ (a type of flower)

unit
tuna
duet
menu
tulip
emu

human
music
usual
computer
unicorn
unicycle

peculiar
cucumber
unique
universe
communicate
solution

Look up each word in the dictionary and read its definition. Write the page number in the computer.

Split these words into syllables.

duet   emu   unique   cucumber   computer

Parse these sentences.

She continuously hummed the school song.

He will cut the cucumber and put it in the Greek salad.

Irregular Plurals

Read each word and illustrate it. If the noun is singular, draw one picture. If the noun is plural, draw more than one picture.

child	woman	foot
women	children	feet
people	person	mouse
sheep	mice	fish
tooth	sheep	fish
teeth	goose	geese

Now join each singular noun to the corresponding plural.

Fill in the missing letters in these words from the spelling list.

p_as__r   __j_m__

as_   _ra__h___er

_as__or_   ___ma

_ul___a   _voc___

__s_et__ll   c__n_e

k___a   l_v_

v_s_   _rm_d_

p_r__h_   __th   n_st_

ask
vase
lava
bath
nasty
sultana

chance
koala
drama
plaster
pyjamas
disaster

piranha
basketball
avocado
armada
passport
grasshopper

Look up each word in the dictionary and read its definition. Write the page number in the basketball.

raft   vase   moustache

llama   answer   armada

Split these words into syllables.

sultana   demand   grasshopper   origami   father

Parse these sentences.

I will be visiting Welsh castles in the holidays.

My father ate a delicious tomato sandwich for lunch.

The Subject of a Sentence

In each sentence, underline the verb(s) in red. Then draw a box around the subject and put a small ‹s› in the corner.

The [birds] ate some seeds.

Sam likes basketball.

The man fell over.

The cat chased a mouse.

Sophie scored the winning goal.

The rancher lassoed the cow.

She sent me an email.

The vase is very old and valuable.

You will be visiting me in the holidays.

The wind blew down an old tree.

Ann ran in the cross-country race.

The rattlesnake shook his tail and hissed.

I made a cake today.

Sue played with her kitten.

The kitten played with Sue.

The seal was swimming close to the beach.

⟨ie⟩

field
chief
piece
brief
shield
grief

relief
frieze
fielder
priest
believe
achieve

diesel
thieves
besiege
audience
briefcase
unbelievable

Put the words in the spelling list into alphabetical order.

1. _____   10. _____
2. _____   11. _____
3. _____   12. _____
4. _____   13. _____
5. _____   14. _____
6. _____   15. _____
7. _____   16. _____
8. _____   17. _____
9. _____   18. _____

Look up each word in the dictionary and read its definition. Write the page number in the shield.

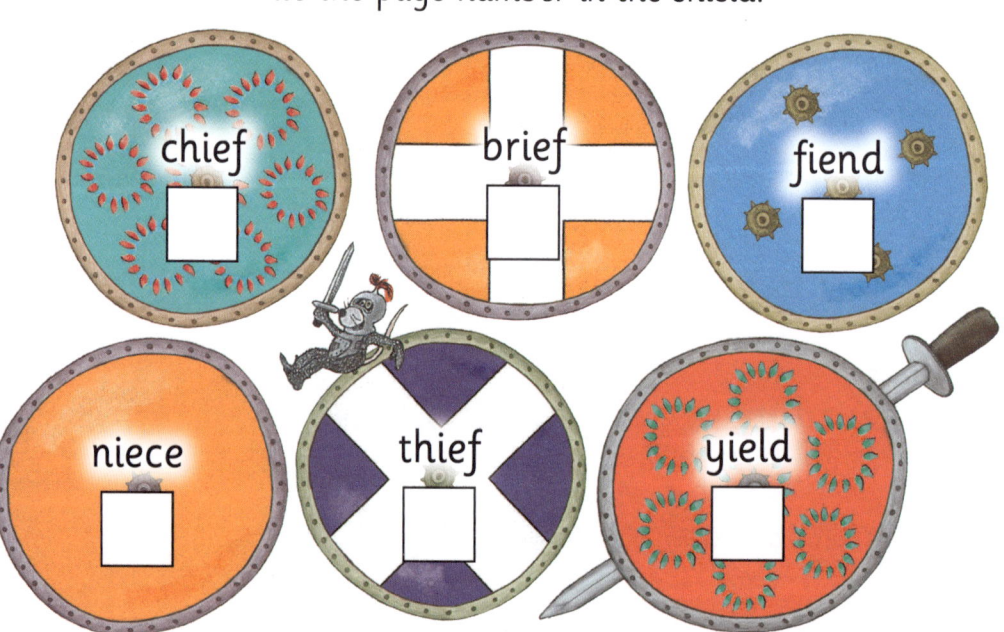

chief   brief   fiend   niece   thief   yield

Split these words into syllables. For words of one syllable add the long or short vowel symbol.

shriek   mantelpiece   diesel   briefcase   grieve

Parse these sentences and identify the subject in each one.

The mighty army was besieging the huge castle.

They carefully painted a beautiful frieze on the tallest wall.

The Object of a Sentence

In each sentence, underline the verb(s) in red. Then find the subject and the object of the sentence. Put a box with a small ‹s› around the subject and a ring with a small ‹o› around the object.

The [cat] chased a (mouse).

The rancher lassoed the cow.

I made a cake today.

Seth kicked the ball.

The lady wrote a letter.

The boy is reading a comic.

The artist painted a portrait.

The dog ate the bone.

He shut the drawer.

Megan opened the door.

Grandma knitted a scarf.

We prepared the salad for lunch.

She plays the flute beautifully.

Joe chased the puppy.

The puppy chased Joe.

I shall be learning a poem for the concert.

When you've finished, help Snake and me to colour the picture.

Put the words in the spelling list into the crossword.

1	abyss
2	myth
3	lynx
4	lyrics
5	syrup
6	idyllic
7	pyramid
8	symbol
9	cymbal
10	system
11	Egypt
12	typical
13	syllable
14	sympathy
15	mystery
16	rhythm
17	acrylic
18	physical

Look up each word in the dictionary and read its definition. Write the page number in the syrup.

Split these words into syllables. For words of one syllable add the long or short vowel symbol.

Olympic   cygnet   system   hymn   pygmy

Parse these sentences and identify the subject in each one.

She will be learning the lyrics for her new song.

We heard mysterious myths about the Egyptian pyramids.

Subject and Object Pronouns

Write the correct pronouns below.

Subject Pronouns		Object Pronouns
_____	1st Person Singular	_____
_____	2nd Person Singular	_____
_____	3rd Person Singular	_____
_____	1st Person Plural	_____
_____	2nd Person Plural	_____
_____	3rd Person Plural	_____

In each pair of sentences, underline the verbs in red and the pronouns in pink. Then decide which pronoun is the subject of the sentence and which is the object.

You hugged Granny. Granny hugged you.
I hit the ball. The ball hit me.
The baby amused her. She amused the baby.
He phoned the school. The school phoned him.
The teacher helped them. They helped the teacher.
We invited some friends. Some friends invited us.
You all saw the animals. The animals saw you all.
It explains everything. That explains it.

Write in the missing pronouns to complete the sentences.

You like horses. Horses like _____ too.
I heard Adam. Adam heard _____.
The boy pushed her. _____ pushed the boy.
The crowd followed them. _____ followed the crowd.
We took the train to the beach. The train took _____ there.

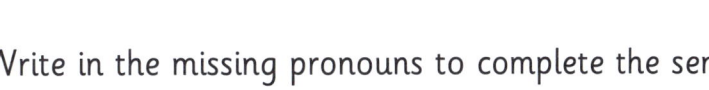

Find the words from the spelling list.
Which one is missing?

a	b	s	t	w	a	d	d	l	e	r	r	y	n
s	w	a	f	t	z	i	n	g	c	h	i	m	f
s	w	a	p	l	e	s	q	u	a	b	b	l	e
g	y	q	u	a	n	t	i	t	y	r	o	u	w
s	q	u	a	l	i	t	y	p	i	n	t	a	x
z	e	u	t	h	s	w	a	n	d	a	y	e	r
s	w	a	m	p	l	e	n	w	a	l	l	e	t
s	w	a	t	c	h	i	n	v	o	i	c	k	u
c	e	i	l	i	n	y	s	q	u	a	l	i	d
w	r	o	t	w	r	i	s	t	w	a	t	c	h
p	h	y	s	i	c	i	a	s	q	u	a	d	n
f	l	i	s	q	u	a	t	h	v	i	x	o	l
w	a	d	d	l	e	w	a	l	l	a	b	y	r
j	e	a	r	y	q	u	a	n	d	a	r	y	v

swap
waft
swamp
wand
wallet
squad

swatch
squat
squalid
quality
wallaby
waddle

squabble
twaddle
quandary
wristwatch
quantity
qualification

Look up each word in the dictionary and read its definition.
Write the page number in the swan.

quality   wasp   squash
wallet   wander   swamp

Split these words into syllables. For words of one syllable add the long or short vowel symbol.

squash   quarry   wander   wallet   twaddle

Parse these sentences and identify the subject in each one.

The swallow swoops high into the sunny sky.

The white swan is floating gracefully along the River Thames.

56

Possessive Pronouns

mine yours his hers ours yours theirs

Read each pair of sentences and then write a new one, using the correct possessive pronoun.

This hat belongs to me.
It is my hat.
It is mine.

This book belongs to us.
It is our book.

_____

This coat belongs to him.
It is his coat.

_____

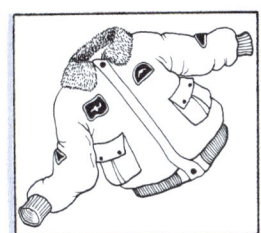

That teddy belongs to you.
It is your teddy.

_____

That dog belongs to you all.
It is your dog.

_____

That cat belongs to them.
It is their cat.

_____

This brush belongs to her.
It is her brush.

_____

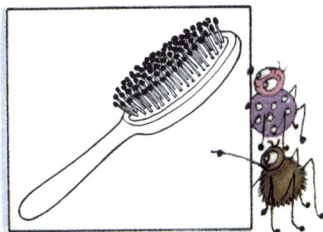

Colour the pictures when you have finished.

⟨au⟩　⟨aw⟩

⟨al⟩

halt
hawk
sauce
haul
thaw
salt

flaw
drawn
laundry
dawdle
already
launch

auburn
awkward
alternative
audition
altogether
awesome

Which words in the spelling list match these descriptions?

1. _____ (it can be added to food)
2. _____ (when snow or ice melts)
3. _____ (clothes to be washed)
4. _____ (another option)
5. _____ (to put a ship in the water)
6. _____ (a reddish brown colour)
7. _____ (a bird of prey)
8. _____ (to stop moving)
9. _____ (to pull with much effort)
10. _____ (clumsy or difficult to use)

Look up each word in the dictionary and read its definition. Write the page number in the clean laundry.

Split these words into syllables.

awkward　autumn　lawnmower　awesome　astronaut

Parse these sentences and identify the subject in each one.

They chalked a giant picture on the tall wall.

The barn owl hooted and called loudly until dawn.

  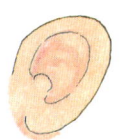 

Homophone Mix-Ups

are	are				
our	our				

Is it '**are**' or '**our**'?
Read each sentence and cross out the incorrect word.

How | are | our | you?

This is | are | our | house.

Javid is in | are | our | team.

Where | are | our | you going on Saturday?

The pencils | are | our | in the cupboard.

The circus acrobats | are | our | very good.

We put the picnic things in | are | our | car.

| Are | Our | dog is very friendly.

Should it be '**are**' or '**our**'?
Complete each sentence by writing in the correct word(s).

We _____ going to the beach at the weekend.

When _____ they arriving?

We stayed at _____ cousin's house in the holidays.

Which blouse _____ you going to wear?

_____ grandma is a very good cook.

Can we go when we have put on _____ coats?

The cakes _____ in the spotty yellow tin.

How _____ _____ friends getting to the zoo tomorrow?

59

Homophones

reed
read
sum
some
blue
blew

brake
break
wood
would
ate
eight

weather
whether
stare
stair
aloud
allowed

Read the words and draw the correct picture in each box.

blew	blue
read	reed
ate	eight

Look up each word in the dictionary and read its definition. Write the page number in the hare with the hair.

right   cell   wear

write   sell   where

Split these words into syllables. For words of one syllable add the long or short vowel symbol.

cell   leak   cymbal   sell   leek   symbol

Parse these sentences and identify the subject in each one.

I am reading a book about reeds.

The wind blew the clouds across the blue sky.

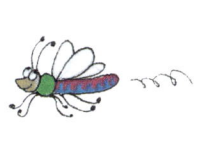  # Homophone Mix-Ups

there _____ _____ _____

their _____ _____ _____

they're _____ _____ _____

Is it 'there', 'their' or 'they're'?
Read each sentence and cross out the incorrect words.

| There | Their | They're | going to cut the cake now.

The twins invited | there | their | they're | friends to the party.

| There | Their | They're | is a spider on the ceiling.

It was so cold they put on | there | their | they're | coats.

Put the chairs back over | there | their | they're |.

On Wednesday | there | their | they're | playing hockey.

Should it be 'there', 'their' or 'they're'?
Complete each sentence by writing in the correct word(s).

They put on _____ boots when it rains.

We went _____ by bus.

When _____ ready, we can go.

_____ is plenty of time before we leave.

They got _____ books out of the locker.

If _____ good, they will get a treat.

_____ are ten children with _____ parents and _____ staying all day.

61

⟨ear⟩
⟨ere⟩ ⟨eer⟩

deer
hear
steer
peer
rear
cheer

here
clear
mere
gearbox
fearful
sneering

interfere
dreary
disappear
smeary
appearance
atmosphere

Fill in the missing letters in these words from the spelling list.

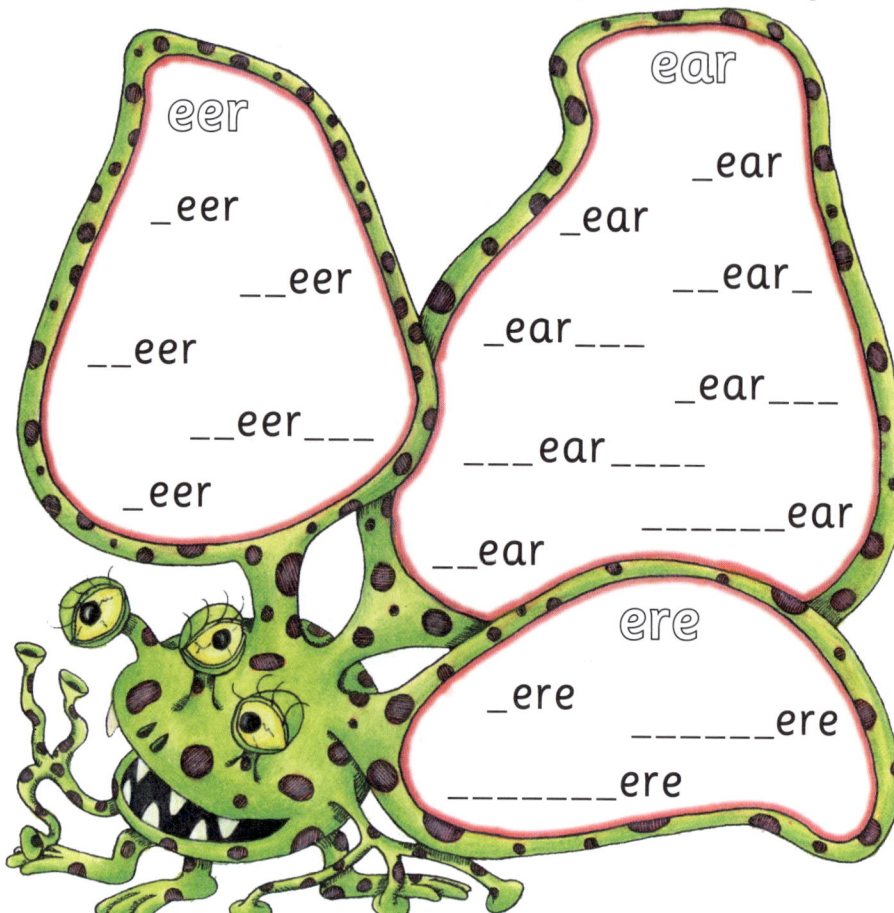

Look up each word in the dictionary and read its definition. Write the page number in the gear.

Split these words into syllables.

cheerful   atmosphere   fearless   nearly   interfere

Parse these sentences and identify the subject in each one.

The red car had a faulty gearbox.

The fearful deer stood hesitantly by the big oak tree.

 # Questions and Exclamations in Speech

Write out the words in the speech bubbles as sentences. Remember to explain who is speaking and to add the correct punctuation. Colour the pictures when you have finished.

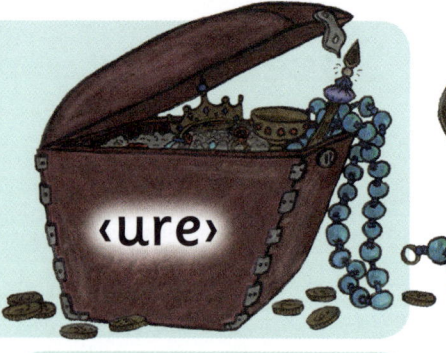

‹ure›

Find the words from the spelling list.
Which one is missing?

o	f	i	x	t	u	r	e	s	s	u	r	e	e
f	e	a	t	u	r	e	w	f	i	g	u	r	e
q	r	t	r	e	a	s	u	r	e	b	l	e	
f	a	i	l	p	r	e	s	s	u	r	e	r	d
l	e	i	s	u	r	e	a	d	j	u	r	e	r
c	o	n	j	u	r	e	m	a	t	u	r	e	s
u	m	e	a	s	u	r	e	m	e	n	t	n	g
l	e	i	s	u	m	o	i	s	t	u	r	e	v
v	u	l	t	u	o	v	c	a	p	t	u	r	e
c	o	m	p	o	s	u	r	e	t	u	r	e	d
f	a	i	l	u	r	e	p	r	e	a	s	u	r
p	u	n	c	t	u	m	a	n	i	c	u	r	e
s	e	c	u	p	l	e	a	s	u	r	e	m	y
v	u	l	t	u	r	e	s	s	e	c	u	r	e

capture
fixture
vulture
feature
puncture
moisture

pressure
leisure
pleasure
treasure
composure
measurement

figure
failure
conjure
mature
secure
manicure

Look up each word in the dictionary and read its definition.
Write the page number in the treasure.

vulture ☐   pleasure ☐   figure ☐

mature ☐   pressure ☐   failure ☐

Split these words into syllables.

pressure   vulture   composure   moisture   fixture

Parse these sentences and identify the subject in each one.

His new bike has a slow puncture.

The mature conjurer produced a huge vulture from the box.

Prefixes

There are many prefixes, but these are nine of the most useful ones.

un- dis- mis- de- semi-
im- re- non- mid-

Which of the prefixes can be added to these root words?
Put the new word underneath. Write a sentence for each word showing their different meanings.

kind
_____

agree
_____

sense
_____

behave
_____

possible
_____

Put the words in the spelling list into the crossword.

1	gnu
2	gnat
3	gnash
4	resign
5	gnaw
6	gnome
7	design
8	align
9	assign
10	gnarled
11	signpost
12	reign
13	feign
14	malign
15	designer
16	benign
17	foreigner
18	poignant

Look up each word in the dictionary and read its definition. Write the page number in the road sign.

Split these words into syllables. For words of one syllable add the long or short vowel symbol.

signpost   gnat   assign   gnome   design

Parse these sentences and identify the subject in each one.

The foreigner saw the broken signpost.

The fierce lion gnashes his teeth and gnaws at the bone.

Collective Nouns

Find the collective noun in each sentence.

A shoal of fish swam into the bay.

The boy picked up a bunch of grapes.

We saw a huge flock of birds in the sky.

There was a huge fleet of ships out at sea.

There is a colony of ants in the garden.

The audience of listeners enjoyed the radio show.

Complete each phrase with a suitable noun.

 a choir of _____   a herd of _____

a bouquet of _____   a team of _____

a crowd of _____   a library of _____

Write a collective noun to describe each of these groups. Colour the pictures when you have finished.

_____   _____   _____

‹ph› ‹gh›

aphid
rough
hyphen
phrase
graphic
laugh

toughest
decipher
enough
phantom
autograph
apostrophe

triumph
amphibian
laughter
coughing
pharmacy
phenomenon

Add ‹ph› or ‹gh› to complete each word and draw a picture.

Dan's dol__in

Lenny's lau__

Fred's __one

Sam's s__ere

Cara's cou__

Anna's am__ibian

Look up each word in the dictionary and read its definition.
Write the page number in the amphibian.

cliff   amphibian   phonic
cough   nephew   phantom

Split these words into syllables.

aphid   roughly   coughing   decipher   phenomenon

Parse these sentences and identify the subject in each one.

The tough Indian elephant laughed triumphantly.

A toad is a warty amphibian.

Sentences and Phrases

Use each phrase in a sentence, underlining the phrase in pencil and the verb in red.
Colour the pictures when you have finished.

the red-haired boy

one sunny morning

a cup of tea

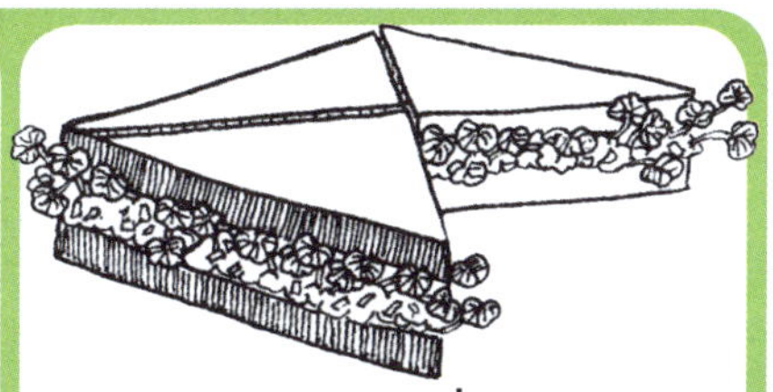

an egg and cress sandwich

out at sea

on the road

⟨air⟩ ⟨ear⟩ ⟨ere⟩ ⟨are⟩

fair
mare
spare
fairy
bare
there

airless
dairy
flare
repair
airport
compare

fanfare
prepare
bearable
hairdresser
somewhere
wherewithal

Which words in the spelling list match these descriptions?

1. _____ (a female horse)
2. _____ (where butter is made)
3. _____ (uncovered or empty)
4. _____ (to fix or mend)
5. _____ (where planes take off)
6. _____ (a short tune on a trumpet)
7. _____ (to get ready)
8. _____ (with light hair or skin)
9. _____ (a small, magical person)
10. _____ (to burst into bright flame suddenly)

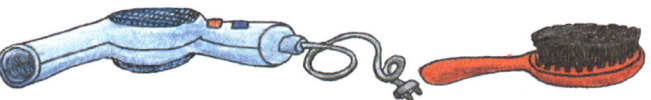

Look up each word in the dictionary and read its definition. Write the page number in the pear.

Split these words into syllables.

bearable   hairdresser   repair   fanfare   somewhere

Parse these sentences and identify the subject in each one.

She is making cheese in the farm dairy.

The brown mare had her young foal with her.

The Subject and Object of a Sentence

In each sentence, underline the verb(s) in red. Find the subject and put a box around it with a small ‹s› in the corner. Then, if there is an object, put a ring around it with a small ‹o› inside.

[s] Zack eats an (ice cream)[o]

Rose paints a picture.

Sam runs quickly.

Lucy is riding a horse.

The dog frightened the man.

We sang happily this morning.

He crashed the car.

The dragon was breathing fire.

The author is writing a novel.

They are singing a song.

Grandpa is sleeping.

She whistles a tune loudly.

The lion climbs the tree.

The woman is taking photos.

The boy watched the monkey.

The monkey watched the boy.

When you've finished, colour in the ice cream with your favourite flavours. My favourite is strawberry!

‹ex›

exit
expect
expel
expert
extra
exist

excuse
except
explain
explore
extract
excite

excellent
expensive
example
exhibition
exhausted
examination

Put the words in the spelling list into alphabetical order.

1. _____   10. _____
2. _____   11. _____
3. _____   12. _____
4. _____   13. _____
5. _____   14. _____
6. _____   15. _____
7. _____   16. _____
8. _____   17. _____
9. _____   18. _____

Look up words beginning with ‹ex› in the dictionary. Find six words that are not in the spelling list and write them below.

_____ _____ _____

_____ _____ _____

Split these words into syllables.

expect   expensive   exit   except   excellent

Parse these sentences and identify the subject in each one.

They looked expectantly at the excellent explorer.

The excited expert is examining the expensive Roman necklace.

Verb Tense Tents

Verbs

For each sentence, underline the verb in red and join the sentence to the correct tense in the tense tent.

- She tunes her violin. → simple present
- She is tuning her violin.
- She tuned her violin.
- She will tune her violin.
- She was tuning her violin.
- She will be tuning her violin.

Tent 1:
- simple past
- simple present
- simple future
- past continuous
- present continuous
- future continuous

Tent 2:
- simple past
- simple present
- simple future
- past continuous
- present continuous
- future continuous

- They pop the balloons.
- They will be popping the balloons.
- They are popping the balloons.
- They popped the balloons.
- They were popping the balloons.
- They will pop the balloons.

- The boat floats on the lake.
- The boat is floating on the lake.
- The boat floated on the lake.
- The boat will float on the lake.
- The boat was floating on the lake.
- The boat will be floating on the lake.

Tent 3:
- simple past
- simple present
- simple future
- past continuous
- present continuous
- future continuous

Spelling Test 1	Spelling Test 2	Spelling Test 3
1.	1.	1.
2.	2.	2.
3.	3.	3.
4.	4.	4.
5.	5.	5.
6.	6.	6.
7.	7.	7.
8.	8.	8.
9.	9.	9.
10.	10.	10.
11.	11.	11.
12.	12.	12.
13.	13.	13.
14.	14.	14.
15.	15.	15.
16.	16.	16.
17.	17.	17.
18.	18.	18.

Spelling Test 4	Spelling Test 5	Spelling Test 6
1.	1.	1.
2.	2.	2.
3.	3.	3.
4.	4.	4.
5.	5.	5.
6.	6.	6.
7.	7.	7.
8.	8.	8.
9.	9.	9.
10.	10.	10.
11.	11.	11.
12.	12.	12.
13.	13.	13.
14.	14.	14.
15.	15.	15.
16.	16.	16.
17.	17.	17.
18.	18.	18.

Spelling Test 7	Spelling Test 8	Spelling Test 9
1.	1.	1.
2.	2.	2.
3.	3.	3.
4.	4.	4.
5.	5.	5.
6.	6.	6.
7.	7.	7.
8.	8.	8.
9.	9.	9.
10.	10.	10.
11.	11.	11.
12.	12.	12.
13.	13.	13.
14.	14.	14.
15.	15.	15.
16.	16.	16.
17.	17.	17.
18.	18.	18.

Spelling Test 10	Spelling Test 11	Spelling Test 12
1.	1.	1.
2.	2.	2.
3.	3.	3.
4.	4.	4.
5.	5.	5.
6.	6.	6.
7.	7.	7.
8.	8.	8.
9.	9.	9.
10.	10.	10.
11.	11.	11.
12.	12.	12.
13.	13.	13.
14.	14.	14.
15.	15.	15.
16.	16.	16.
17.	17.	17.
18.	18.	18.

Spelling Test 13	Spelling Test 14	Spelling Test 15
1.	1.	1.
2.	2.	2.
3.	3.	3.
4.	4.	4.
5.	5.	5.
6.	6.	6.
7.	7.	7.
8.	8.	8.
9.	9.	9.
10.	10.	10.
11.	11.	11.
12.	12.	12.
13.	13.	13.
14.	14.	14.
15.	15.	15.
16.	16.	16.
17.	17.	17.
18.	18.	18.
Spelling Test 16	Spelling Test 17	Spelling Test 18
1.	1.	1.
2.	2.	2.
3.	3.	3.
4.	4.	4.
5.	5.	5.
6.	6.	6.
7.	7.	7.
8.	8.	8.
9.	9.	9.
10.	10.	10.
11.	11.	11.
12.	12.	12.
13.	13.	13.
14.	14.	14.
15.	15.	15.
16.	16.	16.
17.	17.	17.
18.	18.	18.

Spelling Test 19	Spelling Test 20	Spelling Test 21
1.	1.	1.
2.	2.	2.
3.	3.	3.
4.	4.	4.
5.	5.	5.
6.	6.	6.
7.	7.	7.
8.	8.	8.
9.	9.	9.
10.	10.	10.
11.	11.	11.
12.	12.	12.
13.	13.	13.
14.	14.	14.
15.	15.	15.
16.	16.	16.
17.	17.	17.
18.	18.	18.

Spelling Test 22	Spelling Test 23	Spelling Test 24
1.	1.	1.
2.	2.	2.
3.	3.	3.
4.	4.	4.
5.	5.	5.
6.	6.	6.
7.	7.	7.
8.	8.	8.
9.	9.	9.
10.	10.	10.
11.	11.	11.
12.	12.	12.
13.	13.	13.
14.	14.	14.
15.	15.	15.
16.	16.	16.
17.	17.	17.
18.	18.	18.

Spelling Test 25	Spelling Test 26	Spelling Test 27
1.	1.	1.
2.	2.	2.
3.	3.	3.
4.	4.	4.
5.	5.	5.
6.	6.	6.
7.	7.	7.
8.	8.	8.
9.	9.	9.
10.	10.	10.
11.	11.	11.
12.	12.	12.
13.	13.	13.
14.	14.	14.
15.	15.	15.
16.	16.	16.
17.	17.	17.
18.	18.	18.

Spelling Test 28	Spelling Test 29	Spelling Test 30
1.	1.	1.
2.	2.	2.
3.	3.	3.
4.	4.	4.
5.	5.	5.
6.	6.	6.
7.	7.	7.
8.	8.	8.
9.	9.	9.
10.	10.	10.
11.	11.	11.
12.	12.	12.
13.	13.	13.
14.	14.	14.
15.	15.	15.
16.	16.	16.
17.	17.	17.
18.	18.	18.

Spelling Test 31	Spelling Test 32	Spelling Test 33
1.	1.	1.
2.	2.	2.
3.	3.	3.
4.	4.	4.
5.	5.	5.
6.	6.	6.
7.	7.	7.
8.	8.	8.
9.	9.	9.
10.	10.	10.
11.	11.	11.
12.	12.	12.
13.	13.	13.
14.	14.	14.
15.	15.	15.
16.	16.	16.
17.	17.	17.
18.	18.	18.

Spelling Test 34	Spelling Test 35	Spelling Test 36
1.	1.	1.
2.	2.	2.
3.	3.	3.
4.	4.	4.
5.	5.	5.
6.	6.	6.
7.	7.	7.
8.	8.	8.
9.	9.	9.
10.	10.	10.
11.	11.	11.
12.	12.	12.
13.	13.	13.
14.	14.	14.
15.	15.	15.
16.	16.	16.
17.	17.	17.
18.	18.	18.

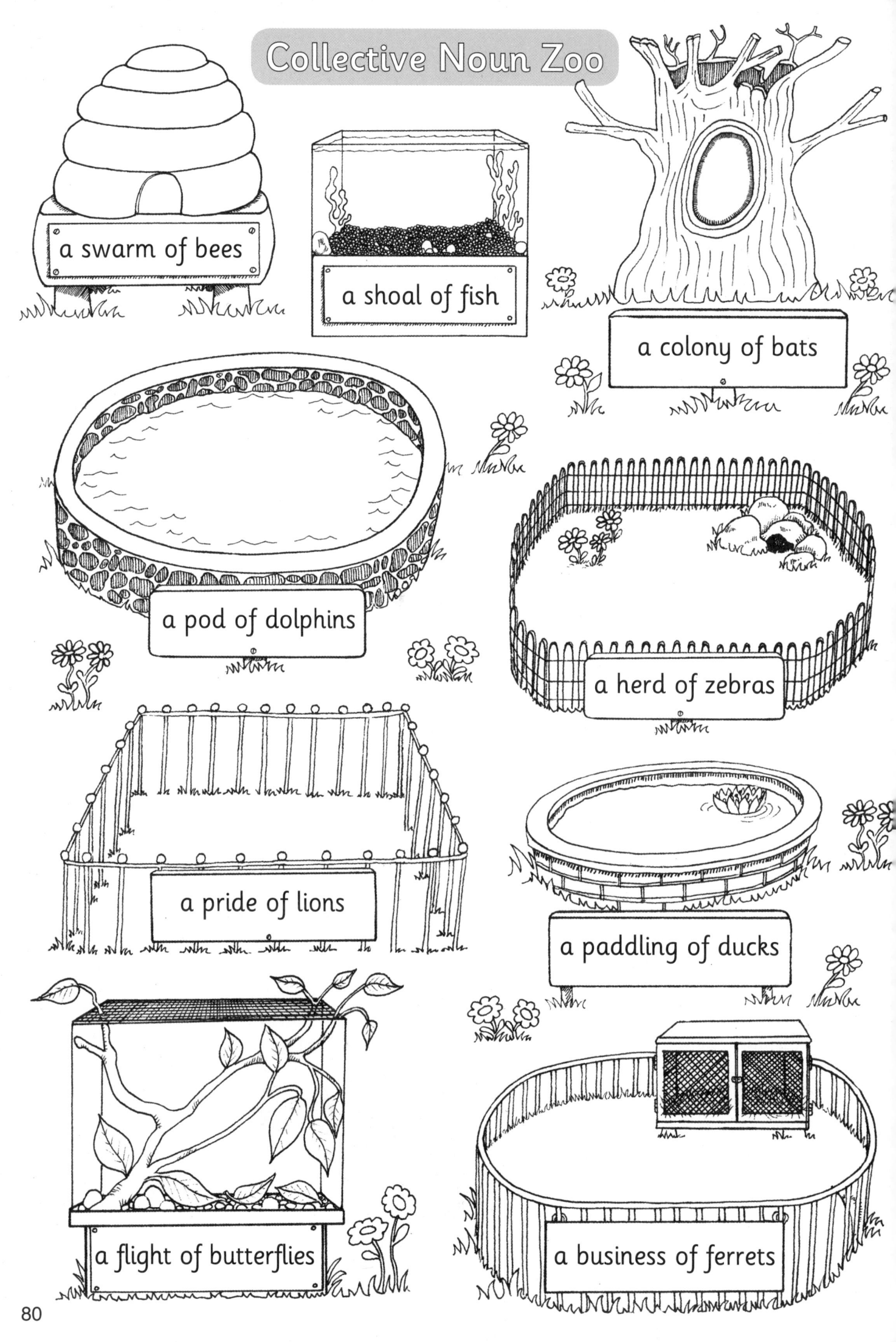